My First Rabbit

Veronica Ross

Chrysalis Children's Books

First published in the UK in 2002 by
🌢 Chrysalis Children's Books
An imprint of Chrysalis Books Group Plc
The Chrysalis Building, Bramley Road, London W10 6SP

Paperback edition first published in 2004
Copyright © Chrysalis Books Group Plc 2002
Text by Veronica Ross

ISBN 1 84138 402 X (hb)
ISBN 1 84458 232 9 (pb)

British Library Cataloguing in Publication Data for this book is
available from the British Library.

Designer: Helen James
Picture researcher: Terry Forshaw
Consultants: Frazer Swift and Nikki Spevack

Printed in China

10 9 8 7 6 5 4 3 2 1

All photography Warren Photographic/Jane Burton with exception of:
11 Frank Lane Picture Agency/M. Rose; 13 Bubbles/Jeannie Woodcock; 19 RSPCA
Photolibrary/Angela Hampton.

Contents

Your pet rabbit

Rabbits look very cute and cuddly, and they are great fun to have as pets. But they do need to be looked after carefully.

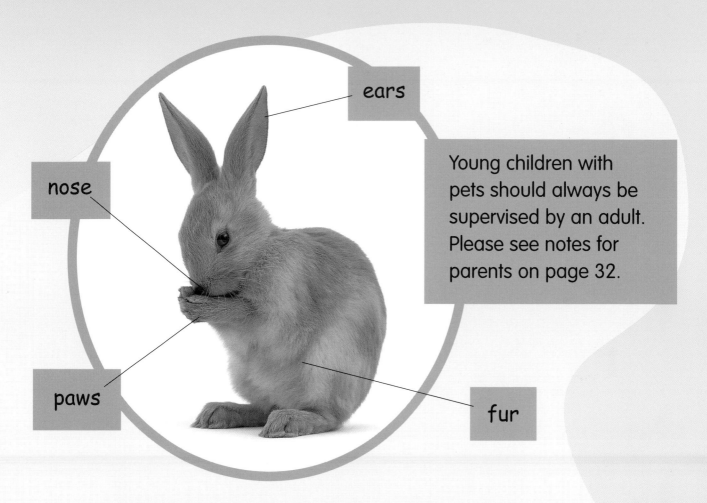

ears

nose

paws

fur

Young children with pets should always be supervised by an adult. Please see notes for parents on page 32.

Rabbits need to eat healthy food. They must have fresh water to drink every day, and plenty of exercise.

When you go on holiday, you will need to find someone who will look after your rabbit while you are away.

What is a rabbit?

Rabbits are mammals. All mammals are warm-blooded and have hair or fur on their bodies. There are many different kinds of rabbits. Some have long, fluffy fur. Other rabbits have large, droopy ears.

Some rabbits have ears that grow so long they touch the floor.

Small rabbits are called dwarf rabbits.

Rabbits have strong, sharp teeth that grow all the time.

This rabbit has very long fur.

Newborn rabbits

Baby rabbits stay close together to keep warm.

Newborn rabbits are small and pink. They do not have any fur. They cannot see or hear, but they can smell.

Baby rabbits are called kittens.

These rabbits are drinking their mother's milk.

When a baby rabbit is three weeks old it has all its fur.

Choosing a rabbit

Rabbits can be bought from pet shops or breeders. Animal shelters are also good places to look for rabbits.

A rabbit should have bright eyes, clean ears and nose, and clean teeth.

Choose a friendly rabbit that looks healthy and lively.

Ask the owner if you can hold the rabbit you like best.

Ask your friends or teachers at school if they know anyone with rabbits that need new homes.

A place to live

A rabbit hutch should have a sleeping area and a living area. Cover the floor with newspaper and sawdust or wood shavings. Put hay in the sleeping area.

Your rabbit will need a food bowl and a drip-feed water bottle.

Put a large hutch (called a run) in the garden so that your rabbit can exercise and eat some fresh grass.

Your rabbit will like being outside.

A hutch can be kept indoors or outdoors. If it is outside make sure that it is sheltered from the wind, rain and sun.

Holding your rabbit

To pick up your rabbit, put one hand under its chest, behind its front legs. Put your other hand under its bottom and lift it up. Put the rabbit down gently. Place its back legs on the floor first.

Hold your pet close to you so that it feels safe.

Be careful with your pet. If you drop it you will hurt it.

Your rabbit will need time to settle into its new home. Leave it for a day before you pick it up.

Feeding your rabbit

Rabbits should have two meals at the same time each day. In the morning, give your pet a bowl of special rabbit food.

Put food in a heavy bowl so your pet cannot knock it over.

Rabbits also enjoy eating dandelion leaves.

In the evening, it will enjoy munching on hard fruit and vegetables, such as pears, apples, carrots and parsnips.

Make sure your pet's water bottle is full all the time.

Always wash fruit and vegetables.

Play time

Leave out boxes and baskets for your rabbit to play with.

Rabbits love to play. They will enjoy hopping about indoors or in the garden.

Keep sharp things and hot drinks out of the way, and don't let your pet chew any wires or cables.

If you're outdoors, make sure that there aren't any gaps in the garden fence or your rabbit will try to escape!

Always stay with your pet when it is outside.

Training your rabbit

You can train
your rabbit to use a
litter tray. Leave the tray where
your rabbit goes to the toilet and
it will learn to go there by itself.

Fill the litter tray
with cat litter or
wood shavings.

Rabbits learn very quickly when they are young.

You can teach your rabbit to come to you. Kneel on the ground and hold some food in your hand. Your rabbit will smell the food and come hopping over.

If your rabbit is naughty, say 'no'. When it stops being naughty, give it a treat, such as a piece of carrot.

Keeping clean...

If the hutch isn't kept clean, it will start to smell. Clear out droppings and wet wood shavings every day. Sweep the hutch once a week and put in fresh straw and wood shavings.

Put your rabbit in its carrying box while you clean the hutch.

Clean the hutch
every two weeks.

Every two weeks scrub the hutch with
soapy water, and spray with special
disinfectant from a pet shop.

Wash your rabbit's
bowl and water
bottle every day.

...and healthy

Rabbits spend a lot of time keeping clean. They use their teeth and paws to pick out dirt that is stuck in their fur.

Rabbits need a block of wood from a pet shop to chew. This stops their teeth growing too long.

This rabbit is cleaning its paws.

Rabbits also like to be groomed, or brushed. Use a soft brush and gently brush your rabbit from its head to its tail.

If you brush your rabbit once a week, its fur will stay healthy and soft.

Grooming is a great way to make friends with your pet.

Making friends

In the wild, rabbits live in groups, so your pet will feel lonely without any friends. Two females from the same family will get on very well.

These two rabbits are sisters.

Dogs and cats may scare your rabbit, so it's best to keep them away from your pet.

If you put a male and a female together they will have babies.

Rabbits and guinea pigs can become best friends if they meet when they are very young.

Visiting the vet

If your rabbit has an upset tummy or runny eyes, ears, nose or mouth it must see a vet at once.

Take your rabbit to the vet once a year for a check-up.

Check your pet every day to make sure that it is healthy.

Your vet will tell you about an operation called neutering. This stops rabbits having babies. Rabbits can have lots of babies and finding homes for them all will be difficult.

A female rabbit can have eight babies in one litter and three litters a year. That's 24 babies to look after!

Words to remember

animal shelter A home for unwanted pets.

breeder A person who sells animals.

droppings Rabbit poo.

groom To brush and comb an animal's fur.

hutch The house where a pet rabbit lives.

kitten A baby rabbit.

litter A group of newborn rabbits.

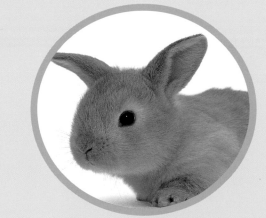

litter tray A rabbit's toilet.

mammal A kind of animal. Mammals have fur on their bodies and feed their babies milk.

vet An animal doctor.

Index

Notes for parents

If you decide to buy a rabbit for your child, it will be your responsibility to ensure that the animal is healthy, happy and safe. You will need to make sure that your child handles the rabbit correctly and does not harm it. Here are some points you should bear in mind before you buy a rabbit:

- Choose your rabbit carefully. Some can be bad-tempered and may bite and kick. Dwarf rabbits are usually easier for children to look after.

- A rabbit costs money to feed. As it gets older, you may have to pay vet's bills as well. Rabbits can live for 12 years.

- You will have to take your rabbit to the vet when it is a year old. The vet will give it an injection against serious diseases.

- Male and female rabbits should be neutered.

- It is best to keep two rabbits together. Two females are ideal, but males and females from the same litter can be kept together if the male is neutered. Two males from the same litter can be kept together, but they must be neutered.

- Rabbits fed on complete diets should not be given mineral supplements unless specifically advised by a vet.

- If you have any questions about looking after your pet rabbit, contact your local vet.